HOPE AND TEARS

ELLIS ISLAND VOICES

HOPE AND TEARS

ELLIS ISLAND VOICES

GWENYTH SWAIN

CALKINS CREEK

Honesdale, Pennsylvania

For information about permission to reproduce selections from this book,
please contact permissions@highlights.com.

Calkins Creek
An Imprint of Boyds Mills Press, Inc.
815 Church Street
Honesdale, Pennsylvania 18431
Printed in China

ISBN: 978-1-59078-765-6

Library of Congress Control Number: 2011940466

First edition

10 9 8 7 6 5 4 3 2 1

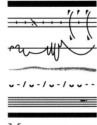

MINNESOTA
STATE ARTS BOARD

This activity is made possible in part by a grant from the Minnesota State Arts Board, through an appropriation by the Minnesota State Legislature and a grant from the National Endowment for the Arts.

Designed by Barbara Grzeslo
Production by Margaret Mosomillo
Titles and text set in Gill Sans
Haikus set in Eames Century Modern

To my grandmother, the late Margaret Hutchinson Coman,
for sharing her memories of Ellis Island

Acknowledgments

I wish to acknowledge the help of the following individuals and institutions in the preparation of this book: Jeffrey Dosik and Barry Moreno, librarians, Bob Hope Memorial Library, Ellis Island Immigration Museum, who both have such wonderful stories to share; Janet Levine, oral historian, Ellis Island Oral History Project; Alexandra Lord, historian, Public Health Service; Dorothy Hartman, director of Education and Public Programs, Save Ellis Island; the Minnesota State Arts Board for generous grant support; Patrick Cullom, archivist, Catholic University of America; the Saint Paul Public Library; Winona State University Library, Winona, Minnesota; Jane Resh Thomas and the Monday Morning Writers Group; author Terri DeGezelle; Joe Flahavan and Doug Nienhuis, teachers, Randolph Heights Elementary School, Saint Paul; the students at Twin Cities Academy, who bring their ideas and interests to the library; editor Carolyn Yoder; and my family.

—GS

Children on the slides and swings, Ellis Island, 1924.

Contents

Thank you for supporting the
Homewood Public Library!

Title: My big fat zombie
goldfish. Any fin is possible
Item ID: 31311005486497
Date due: 11/5/2018,23:59

Title: Hope and tears : Ellis
Island voices
Item ID: 31311004977058
Date due: 11/5/2018,23:59

Nearing the island:

Ellis—place of hope and tears—

and meetings with joy

When the door opens
to this new land, watch me race
right in, barefooted

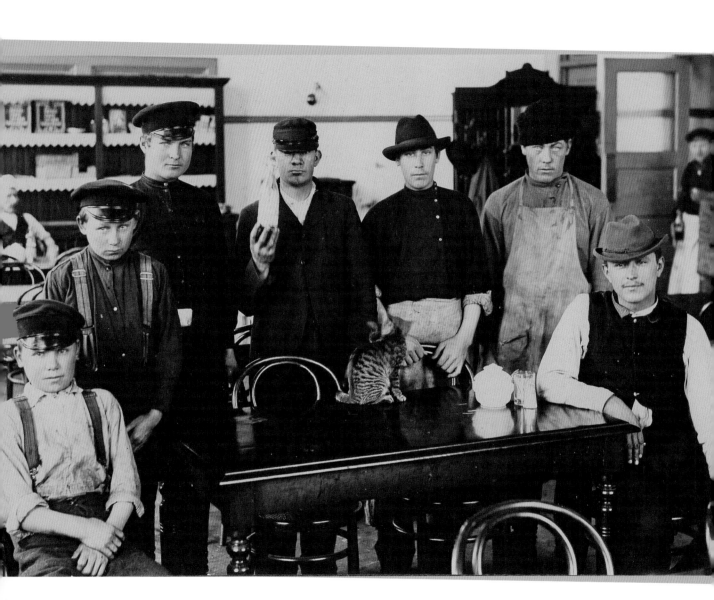

Wear your best hat for
the never-ending waiting . . .
this is history!

Ellis Island, about 1905, with its cluster of red-brick and limestone immigration buildings, sits in New York Bay.

Introduction

Maybe you've heard of Ellis Island before. It once was the largest, busiest immigration point in the United States. Between 1892 and its closing in 1954, an estimated twelve million immigrants passed through this small island in New York Bay on their way to becoming American citizens. One-quarter of all Americans can trace some part of their ancestry to this place.

For me, Ellis Island is a collection of voices. A long time ago, my grandmother shared her memories of visiting the island as a girl in the early 1900s. Grandma had gone there as a tourist, and she mainly remembered the immense crowds. Her visit took place sometime during the peak years of immigration on Ellis (1903–1914), when as many as five thousand people might have passed through in a single day.

When I visited Ellis Island nearly a century later, I heard more stories at the island's Oral History Division, where countless interviews are stored. I also went to the Ellis Island Library, with its wonderful collections of documents and photographs.

The monologues, dialogues, prose poems, and letters that follow grew out of these experiences. Each one can be read silently or performed as a miniplay. Each one reflects the experience of a different person whose life somehow intersected with Ellis Island. Along with these fiction pieces are short factual essays on parts of Ellis Island life and history. Together, they paint a picture of a real place, vital to our history, and filled with hope and tears.

CHAPTER ONE

Ellis Islands

View of Ellis Island, about 1920, showing not one but three separate islands. Two islands in the foreground have since been made into one.

The name *Ellis Island* is singular, as if it were just one place. But it's really plural, a combination of islands.

Originally, it was small and flat. Only sea gulls lived there. Lenni Lenape Indians paddled to the tiny island to fish and find oysters. They called it *Kioshk*, or Gull Island, and they were careful to time their visits. At high tide, they sometimes got wet.

Later, in the 1600s, members of the Dutch West India Company in Nieuw Amsterdam (which later became New York) purchased two islands from the Indians. The bigger one is now known as Liberty Island, while the smaller one is called Ellis. The Dutch left the smaller island undisturbed, except to gather oysters there.

Over the years, the island was owned by several different people. In 1774, it was sold to Samuel Ellis, but by 1785, he was trying to get rid of it. The place didn't have the greatest reputation. It had earned the nickname "Gibbet Island" some years before, when pirates were hanged there, on a gibbet, to die.

When the United States government needed to build a fort to defend New York City against a possible British attack in the years before the War of 1812, Mr. Ellis's heirs finally found a buyer. Ellis Island, as people were calling it then, was flat and wet. The government decided to build it up. Workers used landfill—dirt brought in by boat—to raise the island's level and increase its size. Fort Gibson was built on top of the dirt, but the new fort was never attacked.

By 1890, there was no longer any need to defend New York City from British attack. But the need for a good place to process, or check over, immigrants had grown by leaps and bounds. Ellis Island was the perfect spot for a new immigration center.

A channel, deep enough for ferry boats to dock, was created. A grand pinewood immigration station sprouted up in 1892. Some compared the building to an elegant resort hotel. But on the morning of June 15, 1897, that wooden immigration station burned to the ground. Officials quickly decided to rebuild using fireproof brick and limestone. The grand red-and-white building opened in 1900. It's still standing today but on a much bigger piece of land.

Here's how the island grew: First, in 1898 the main island (called Island One) was joined by another island, called Island Two. This island soon housed a hospital for sick immigrants. In 1912, a second hospital on yet another island (Island Three) was completed. The three islands were linked by a narrow spit of land with a covered walkway. Fill for the islands came in part from dirt removed to make way for New York City's subway system. Even more dirt filled the space between the two hospital islands in the 1920s.

Today, the Ellis Island complex has grown to 27.5 acres. The original island, home to sea gulls and not much else, was only a little more than three acres. In an odd arrangement, the United States Supreme Court ruled in 1998 that the state of New Jersey controls the landfill areas, while the state of New York controls the original island. But who can really own a place with so many names, so many purposes, and so many voices still carried on the winds?

The Lenni Lenape were the first known human visitors to the island they called Kioshk. The sea gulls came before them and are still there.

Pilapeu, Lenni Lenape Boy
(late 1500s)

"Too small."

Always before, when I asked to go to Kioshk, they would say this.

"You won't catch fish with those skinny arms."

Now I'm wedged in the dugout's bottom,

small enough to fit next to the nets and digging sticks.

I feel the tide's push-pull as we leave Mannahatta behind.

There's good fishing along the river that flows both ways.

But even better catches in the great salt sea.

Soon we glide onto a beach studded with shells.

I scramble from the dugout, basket in hand.

The men and older boys get to work.

I wade with my cousin into the slow shallows and begin the hunt.

Shells fill our basket slow but sure.

As the sun sinks, I help pull in the heavy nets.

And when we push off, the dugout sits low.

This time, someone hands me a paddle.

"Skinny arms, but strong."

I slice the water.

But before Kioshk slips from view,

I turn to say "*Wanishi.*"

Thank you, small island, for all you have to give.

Jasper, Dutch Colonist

(about 1630)

Dear Maartje,

A ship sails for home, and this news I send.

My health is fair, but my beard goes untrimmed.

You would take me for a bear.

The colony is in goodly spirits and growing, too.

This year past, for "certain cargoes or parcels of goods,"

the native folk did sell us bits of land.

At first I feared we'd paid too dear.

One nearly disappears at high tide.

I took a skiff and set out to explore.

I know water better than land.

Something told me to wade into an old tide pool.

And there I found oysters—half-buried treasure.

I only wish that you, with your black cookery pot, were here.

You'd stew them—in butter, wine, and rare orange peel—

till they'd melt in my mouth.

The memory of you was on my tongue

as I stood on that island, oyster in hand.

I called your name, but only sea gulls answered.

Until another ship brings you, and your cookery pot,

I remain your loving husband,

Jasper

t' Fort nieuw Amsterdam op de Manhatans

This image of Nieuw Amsterdam—later named Manhattan—
shows how important water was to Europeans. In 1630, the
Dutch in Nieuw Amsterdam bought Kioshk from the Lenni
Lenape, eventually renaming it Little Oyster Island.

17

In 1778, when this map of New York was made, a merchant named Samuel Ellis owned the small island near the lower left corner ("Bucking I."). Samuel Ellis's story starts with a real advertisement from an early New York City newspaper.

"TO BE SOLD
By Samuel Ellis,
NO. 1 GREENWICH STREET,
AT THE NORTH RIVER NEAR THE
BEAR MARKET,
That pleasant situated Island,
CALLED
Oyster Island,
LYING IN NEW YORK BAY,
near Powle's Hook,
TOGETHER WITH ALL ITS IMPROVEMENTS,
WHICH ARE CONSIDERABLE."

Samuel Ellis, Tavern Owner
(1785)

The notice gives a fair accounting, while not telling all.

Truth is, I've been anchored to this place too long.

My island is indeed pleasant situated, yet powerful strange.

It won't hold seed long enough to grow a tree,

but it holds tight to memories.

The rum in my tavern is good,

and still no one cares to drink it.

Years after the last pirate was hanged on the gibbet,

the memory of the noose lingers here.

Some years back, I found a boat adrift.

Pulling it to shore, I heard voices floating from its empty hull.

Dutch or Indian, I couldn't say.

Nearly sat me in the surf, it shocked me so.

I sell wine and spirits,

but there are spirits here that can't be corked in a bottle.

Some are carried on the winds.

If you should hear them moan, pray don't tell a soul.

The notice in the paper says all a buyer needs to know.

I'll entertain any reasonable offer,

for I've made my memories here and am ready to float free.

David, New York Subway Worker
(early 1900s)

I didn't know, when I came through immigration,
that I would end up here, digging holes.
Who could have told me?
No one back in Gwynedd or the whole of north Wales.
No one there ever dreamed of a city so big or so crowded.
Here, there's not enough room for all of us to be up top,
    where the sun shines.
I spend my days down where it's dark,
sifting through mud and sand, blasting through rock.
I'm making tunnels for a great train—a sub-way, they call it—
to carry people under the ground.
And me, who came to America to get out of the mines.
Down here, I've found no coal, but sharp Indian spearpoints.
I've hit my shovel on jugs from the days of General Washington.
The deeper I go, the older this new place gets.
What do they do with the dirt? I wonder.
I dig it all day,
put it in buckets.
When it rises up from this hole, where does it go?
I swear I've dug enough to build a whole new city,
a whole new country, a whole new world.
Godspeed, dirt.
I bid you Godspeed and plenty of sunshine,
wherever you may land.

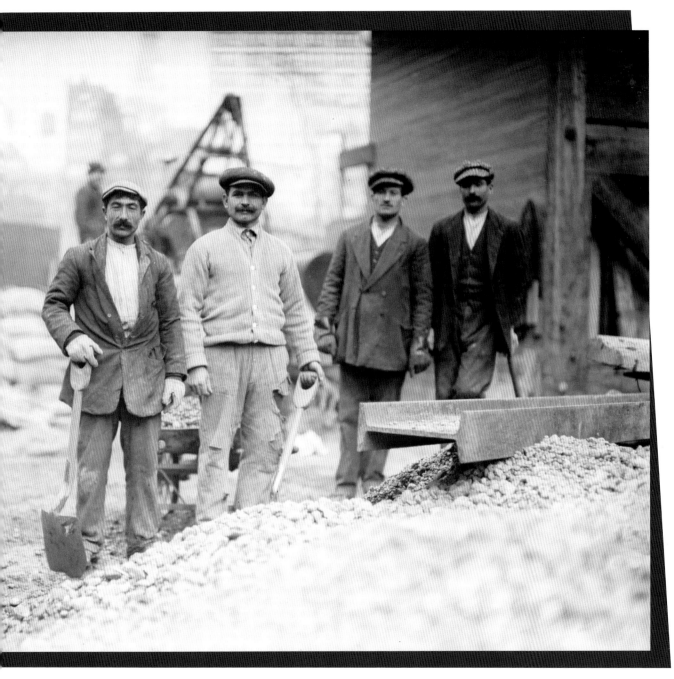

Many who helped build the New York subway were immigrants.
Because dirt removed during construction was used to enlarge
Ellis Island, it's fair to say that immigrants built the island.

CHAPTER TWO

Arrivals

Immigrants walking up the gangplank to the dock at
Ellis Island, early 1900s.

Emigrants from Europe on board a ship head to America around the early 1900s.

Ellis Island processed its first immigrant, fifteen-year-old Annie Moore from Ireland, on January 1, 1892. Millions of immigrants followed, with nearly twelve thousand arriving in a single day in 1907. In many ways, Annie Moore wasn't typical of the immigrants who passed through Ellis Island. By then, even though many Irish still came to America, they were no longer the largest group arriving from Europe.

Ellis Island's immigrants arrived from many countries, including Russia, Italy, Germany, Hungary, Czechoslovakia, Denmark, and Armenia, just to name a few. For nearly all, the journey to America was an anxious time. Depending on the ship's age and condition, crossing the Atlantic Ocean from a European port might take five days . . . or five weeks. Once travelers arrived in New York Harbor, the waiting game continued. "[W]e glided up the still waters of the harbour," one man remembered. "The whole prow was a black mass of passengers staring at the ferry-boats, the distant factories, and sky-scrapers."

Doctors from the Public Health Service, based on Ellis Island, boarded immigrant ships in New York Harbor to check for contagious diseases. They examined first- and second-class passengers for any additional medical conditions that might make them poor bets as immigrants. After healthy first- and second-class passengers got off the ship, third-class, or steerage, passengers were led to barges. These barges would take them away from New York City's docks to Ellis Island, where their true arrival as Americans would begin.

Annie Moore, whose statue can be seen today at Ellis Island, was officially the island's first immigrant. She came from Ireland with her brothers Phillip and Anthony on January 1, 1892— her fifteenth birthday.

Annie Moore, Irish Immigrant

(1892)

Would you warrant it?

So far, I've waited two whole years.

Not until this November could our parents pay the passage.

That's two years of living with Auntie.

Two years of being a sort of mother to Phillip and Anthony,

but not near so good a mother as our own.

Two years to wonder: will my parents know me, with all I've grown?

Now, after twelve days on this ship, crossing from Ireland,

I'm waiting for the end of waiting.

It's daybreak, sun spilling over the harbor.

I hear we're to be heaved onto smaller boats.

Pulling Phillip and Anthony behind, I make for the first one.

I'm running toward the end of waiting.

At last our barge bumps the dock by a tall building—

like a grand hotel, but all of wood and glass and smelling of fresh paint and sap.

"Ladies first!" someone calls.

And *hop!* All of a hurry, here I am, at the head of the line.

I trip over a gangplank that rocks against the shore.

There are cheers, and a crowd presses in.

A hundred tin whistles sound.

A priest gives me a blessing, bless my soul!

Someone thrusts a gold piece into my hands.

A man with a large mustache hands me a certificate.

All this just because I'm the first person through this place!

Lovely gifts, I'm sure.

But I know what waits within.

Our parents . . . the best present of all.

Immigrant ships entered New York Harbor to let off first- and second-class passengers. Passengers in third class, who still had to go through Ellis Island, got a sneak preview of the city many would soon call home.

Anatole, Greek Immigrant

(1919)

From: Anatole1919@gmail.com

To: fetagirl98@caboose.net

Date: Feb. 12, 2010

Subject: Your history students

Thalia dear,

A nice lady was reading me your questions.

Now she types my answers.

First, you ask how I came here.

Well, I was to go to Chicago, to live with cousin Miklos.

But after we steamed into New York Harbor . . .

Well, how could I turn my back on such beauty?

We arrived after midnight.

Shouting woke me—and everyone else.

"America! America!"

We stood at the rails,

the electric lights twinkling like so many stars.

Soon we were near enough to skyscrapers

I thought I could grab one.

The way the Woolworth Building reached to the sky.

The way the windows glittered orange in the new day's sun.

Forget Athens.

Forget Chicago.

From the very first sight,

I ♥ New York.

Nearly as much as I ♥ you.

Be a good girl.

Come visit soon.

XOX –Papou Anatole

Elizabeth Martin, Hungarian Immigrant

(1919)

I met the Liberty Lady on Christmas Eve.

She was there, waiting for us, when we arrived from Hungary.

The sun was sinking, but she lit the harbor for me.

"Ellis," the deckhands said, helping us and our bundles onto barges.

After minutes that seemed like hours,

we spilled onto shore in a fearful, tearful crowd.

Then someone called, and we all followed.

Weren't we good sheep?

Our parents, hustling us up brightly lit stairs,

were too full of worry to remember the date.

But someone at this place understood a child's heart.

Red ribbons and green garlands hung everywhere.

A large, jolly fat man sat grinning.

"Santa Claus," a woman told me, as if I should know.

He wasn't like our Saint Nicholas.

Everyone knew Saint Nick was just a man from the village,

with a long walking stick and a sack on his back.

This man wore a uniform of red

and a beard as white as fresh linens.

He had gifts for us children.

Baby dolls for the girls and teddy bears for the boys.

Oh, how I wished for a teddy bear.

But Santa Claus didn't speak Hungarian.

Try as I might, I couldn't make my wishes known.

I took the doll.

And what do you think I bought when I earned my first American dollar?

The teddy bear right here, in my arms.

Yes, I still have him, after all these years.

We're a little frayed at the edges, we two,

but American, through and through.

Much like the immigrant children in this photograph, Elizabeth Martin, a young Hungarian immigrant, came to America at Christmastime 1919. Someone in her family had measles, so she was detained on Ellis Island for twenty days—including Christmas Eve. Elizabeth was thrilled by the Ellis Island Christmas celebration but disappointed that Santa gave her a baby doll, and not a teddy bear.

From ferries and barges, immigrants arriving on Ellis Island were organized by men called groupers. Because immigrants often did not speak English, groupers had a difficult job. Many immigrants—like this girl in the early 1920s—were scared of them.

Horace, a Grouper

(early 1920s)

I call out.

The girl freezes.

She's caught on the barge's deck,

bundle held close,

fear in her eyes.

I call out again.

But nothing moves her.

"Gee! Gee! Whup!" the other groupers yell.

"Move along, cattle!" is what they mean.

They bark when you stumble,

growl when you freeze,

poke until you moan.

But what good does it do to treat you worse than dirt?

Will it make you find your place in line faster?

As my mama always says,

"Life is short, but candy is sweet."

So, from my coat pocket, I pull a sweet taffy,

bend down to the girl with her bundle,

and gently coax.

Before I know it, her little hand is in mine.

CHAPTER THREE

Inspections

An inspector sits at a high desk while immigrants face him and do their best to answer his questions correctly.

Arriving at Ellis Island, immigrants had already passed through a number of inspections. The steamship companies were supposed to do their best to sort out any "undesirable" immigrants before they got to America. Until the 1920s, immigrants did not need passports to board a ship, but they did have to show that they were healthy. Doctors inspected them before they left ports in Europe as well as on shipboard, making notes on inspection cards. Immigrants carried these cards with them to show the doctors on Ellis Island. Pinned to their clothing before arrival was another card, called a boarding tag, which was given to immigration officials.

Once their feet touched the ground on Ellis Island, immigrants were sorted into groups of about thirty. Women and children were grouped separately from men, but all group members were passengers of the same ship. Each immigrant—often carrying a large bundle or bag—stood in a line that made its way to the ground floor of the main building on Island One.

Upon entering the building, immigrants stood before a United States Public Health Service doctor. Any immigrant made breathless by the short walk from the dock was suspected of hiding illness. Those who limped also were pulled aside. Immigrants removed their hats so doctors could inspect for lice or scalp diseases, such as favus. Farther along the inspection line, still more doctors turned up the eyelids of each immigrant, looking for trachoma, a contagious eye disease. Some of the doctors used their fingers. Others used small metal hooks more commonly used to button boots.

If an immigrant showed signs of disease (either mental or physical), the doctor took a piece of chalk and made a mark on the immigrant's clothing. The mark was meant to tell other doctors in nearby examination rooms what was wrong. *H* stood for "heart"; *L* for "lameness"; *X* for "suspected mental illness."

Those who passed "line" inspections by doctors were then directed up the stairs and into lines stretching across the Registry Room floor. At the far end of the room, the immigrant could see a row of inspectors sitting at high wooden desks. These inspectors first checked off the immigrant's name and number (from the boarding tag) against a long list called a ship's manifest.

Then inspectors questioned immigrants, looking for any legal reason not to admit them. For example, immigrants were required to have a certain amount of money (about twenty dollars) in order to enter the country. Beginning in 1917, immigrants had to pass a test to prove that they could read. They might have been turned away if they claimed to have a job already lined up in their new home. Such arrangements could have stopped current American citizens from finding work.

For those who passed inspection, Ellis Island was a short stop (three to five hours on average) on the long journey toward becoming American. But being short didn't make the Ellis Island experience any less frightening.

Margaret, English Immigrant

(early 1900s)

Dear Diary,

We pushed up broad stairs to a brick and stone building,

red and cream, like London's Albert Hall.

A tall man in uniform stood ahead.

He looked like a soldier, but a woman called him "doctor" and he answered.

Soon he was leaning over the girl in front of me.

She's a baker's helper from Bristol.

We'd talked, you know, about this and that.

The doctor didn't want to get to know her, though.

He pulled a hook from his pocket, and I nearly cried out.

I know that kind of hook well, I do.

It's meant for boots with buttons, not Bristol bakers.

In a flash, the doctor used it to pry up her eyelids.

He sighed, he frowned, and that girl sank to the ground.

I heard him say "trachoma" and knew the worst.

It's a contagious disease, can make you blind sometimes.

Always, it keeps you out of America, no matter how you want in.

Back to Bristol she'll be going.

Sure, that doctor tried to catch me with his ugly metal hook.

But when I passed inspection,

I slipped through his net.

All the same, Diary dear,

I'll be buying boots with laces from this day on.

Immigrants have their eyes examined by doctors on Ellis Island. Those who had trachoma, a contagious eye disease, were turned away.

Wanda, German Bohemian Immigrant
(1911)

Mama sits silent on the bench.

Even though Papa is waiting to take us to our new home,

I know she worries: will America let her in, nearly deaf as she is?

Since I'm the oldest child, I watch over us all.

We're too excited for breakfast.

And who knows how long until lunch?

We wait, stomachs growling.

Jakob pats Mama's shoulder.

Astrid and Minna play at paper dolls.

Olga and Felix nap.

Hans and Hilda jab each other, until I give them the eye.

It's easy to forget about baby Ado, always quiet and full of smiles.

So when I finally remember not to forget, *he's gone!*

I scan the crowd this way, then that,

desperate for some sign of his red-cheeked, round face.

Down on my knees, I search through a forest of feet.

I'm hunting for a good crawler.

Frantic, now, I have Jakob make a cradle with his hands.

Then I put one foot up, peering over that crowd.

At last I see him!

Ado, too, is being held high.

He smiles and waves a chubby hand.

The man holding him sees me wave, too.

Then Ado starts his long journey back,

passing from burly hands to burly hands across that great room.

Yes, the room is crowded.

Yes, we are filled with worries.

But when Ado drops into my arms,
we're all one family in that big, big room,
together still.

In the Registry Room in the early 1900s, lines of people await their immigration inspections.

A number of inspectors on Ellis Island were once immigrants. They were particularly valuable members of the staff because they often could speak several languages. This prose poem is about a real inspector, Syrian-born Najeeb Abreely.

Najeeb Abreely, Immigrant Inspector
(1890s)

When they see my uniform, they think I'm after them.

"Gendarme!" "Al-shurta!" "Police!"

I see the fear in their faces, and I understand.

I use words to soothe their fears.

The first words are my name.

I stab my chest with a finger.

"Inspector Najeeb Abreely."

I point to them.

"What is your name?"

"Votre nom?"

"Shismak?"

The other questions are easier to ask, easier to answer,

once we know each other's names.

Tell me:

Where are you from?

Where are you going?

What is your story?

I have the power to let you in or keep you out.

But understand this:

I have walked in your shoes.

I am Najeeb Abreely, American.

But I am an immigrant, too.

Jarek, Polish Immigrant
(1920s)

The man at the high desk is asking questions.

"Name?"

I whisper an answer.

"Name?" he says, louder now.

This time I manage a mumble.

He motions impatiently for me to show him my tag,

and I hold it up for all to see.

The man makes a note, asks a question through an interpreter, then nods.

"Next!" he yells.

And I'm done.

The paper tag has set me free!

As I go down the stairs, I still hold it tight.

Everything I need is on this slip of paper.

Maybe Father won't know me.

But he does know my name.

He left home when I was just a baby.

But he knows the ship I came on.

He always meant to send for me, or so his letters said.

And now I'm here, ready to pass *his* inspection.

Ready to be his son at last.

INSPECTION CARD

(Immigrants and Steerage Passengers).

The East-Asiatic Company, Limited.
BALTIC AMERICA LINE.

Port of departure, DANZIG.
Name of ship, _S. S. Estonia_
Name of Immigrant, _Izacki, Icek_
Date of departure,
Last residence, _Poland_

Inspected and passed ad DANZIG.	Passed at quarantine, port of	Passed by Immigration Bureau
	U.S.	port of
UNITED STATES PUBLIC HEALTH SERVICE	SENT TO HOSPITAL DEC 4 1925	
Seal Stamp of Consular or Medical Officer	(Date).	(Date).

(The following to be filled in by ship's surgeon or agent prior to or after embarcation).

Ship's list or manifest _10_   No. on ship's list or manifest _15_

Berth No.	Steamship inspection	1st day.	1	2	3	4	5	6	7	8	9	10	11	12	13	14	15	16	17	18	19

No. 37c. 5000. 5. 24.

All immigrants at Ellis Island had to carry tags like these to show inspectors.

Margaret Batchelder, Immigrant Inspector
(1903)

To the Honorable Theodore Roosevelt, President of the United States:

Dear Sir,

Knowing of your interest in immigrants,

I am writing to tell you of my work.

The other inspectors—all men—

say we women cannot question immigrants in the grand hall.

Women, they say, aren't suited for such detailed work.

At first we took offense.

But we soon saw it as an opportunity.

The man inspector, high at his desk,

checking manifests and records,

misses so much.

The man inspector is diligent indeed,

but he rarely *talks* to the immigrants.

When immigrant women and girls arrive on these shores,

they are excited, yes, but frightened, too.

Can a man truly know how they feel?

I think not.

So we women do what needs no translation:

We smile in welcome when they land on the Ellis Island dock.

In whatever language, we try to be a help and a comfort.

It's the best work I can imagine.

I hope that you agree.

Yours most respectfully,

Margaret Batchelder

Beginning in 1903, a small number of women, including one named Margaret Batchelder, were hired as immigrant inspectors. They worked mainly with newly arrived women and children on the Ellis Island dock.

Arnold Weiss, Russian Immigrant

(1930s)

Have you seen the movies starring that puppet Charlie McCarthy?

In my favorite, he's part of a circus.

The circus owner says, "You can't cheat an honest man."

But I know that's not true.

You can cheat—or at least trick—an honest immigration man.

I did it once, not so long ago.

We were at Ellis Island, my mother and I.

We had come from Russia, where Jews were treated horribly.

We were making our escape to a better life.

But first, the inspector said, my mother had to take a test.

"But she knows no English," I told him.

"Then let her take it in Yiddish," the inspector replied,

for he was an honest man.

He pulled out a *siddur*.

I wonder, do you know what that is?

A Jewish book. A prayer book.

A book that, no matter what the language, my dear mother couldn't read.

Here was a hurdle Mother couldn't leap alone.

It stood between her and America.

I saw the passage the inspector wanted her to read.

And quick as a wink, I read those lines silently, inside my head.

Then I slipped under the desk, unnoticed.

No one, save my mother,

heard the words I whispered softly, telling her just what to say.

Her jaws moved like that puppet's, like Charlie McCarthy's.

And loud as she could, she repeated each Yiddish phrase.

We *did* cheat an honest man.

And I've never regretted it to this day!

Wearing a tag for a railroad journey, this woman waits at Ellis Island in the 1920s. Arnold Weiss, a young Russian Jew, remembered his own mother's ordeal on the island in 1921 in an oral history interview. Arnold's memories serve as the basis for this story. Charlie McCarthy was the name of a ventriloquist's dummy who appeared in many movies, including one called You Can't Cheat an Honest Man.

CHAPTER FOUR

Island of Hope, Island of Tears

An Italian immigrant family, poised between hope and tears.
As one immigrant said, "There's more tears in Ellis Island to
ten people than, say, to a hundred people elsewhere. There is
all of these tears, everybody has tears."

Children at the contagious-disease hospital on Ellis Island learned basket weaving during their recovery.

After inspection, most immigrants left the Registry Room, going downstairs to meet relatives, find baggage, exchange foreign money for U.S. dollars, or buy train tickets for longer journeys. But not all immigrants passed inspections. Those who were pulled out of line for any reason, legal or medical, had to wait in detention.

Even those who passed inspections might have to wait. Women and girls traveling alone were not allowed to leave the island until a male relative came to claim them. Families with members who were ill (and staying at the island's hospitals) often stayed in detention until everyone was healthy and ready to travel together.

Some found the waiting easy. Others found it painfully hard. Most were mystified by Ellis Island—its food, its rules, and its hard beds. Perhaps those who were sick with contagious diseases suffered most. Beginning in 1912, they were treated on Island Three, and the sickest among them could not have any visitors.

Some arrivals were labeled "likely to become public charges," an official term covering a wide range of people and circumstances. These included young women traveling alone or traveling with children born outside of marriage; people arriving without money or with no clear means of support; people who were mentally ill; and those with disabilities (such as blindness or lameness) or with infectious diseases (such as trachoma or tuberculosis). Immigrants who were likely to require help from the government in order to survive were often brought before the Board of Special Inquiry. When the final decision came, some repacked their bundles and waited for the next ship home.

Sven, Norwegian Immigrant

(early 1900s)

"Stay with it!" my mother says.

"Don't let it out of your sight, Sven!"

So, I'm stuck, like Robinson Crusoe on his island.

Only it's me on our trunk.

Other people, they have soft bundles.

They can plump up their worldly goods, pillow-fashion, and get a good rest.

But our trunk is straight and hard.

It's pretty, all the same, with Mother's rosemaling.

I study the perfectly painted swirls and lines,

thinking of how Mother straightens my collar,

even when I'm sure it's already straight.

To pass the time, I picture everything inside.

Our trunk holds jewelry, the family Bible,

sheets, pillowcases, and a few teacups

wound up in paper and packed in sawdust.

There's even a bottle of *brennevin*—

home-brewed brandy—wrapped in a pillow.

And feather mattresses rolled up tight, because Father said.

Americans know a lot, he writes, but they don't know how to sleep.

I'm not American yet.

I've been up since someone called out "New York!" just past midnight.

Suddenly, without even knowing it, I slip off to sleep.

Soon, Mother is kicking my feet.

"Up, Sven, up!"

She tries to sound angry, but there's a smile just behind her scowl.

The trunk is still here, and so am I.

Best of all, Mother holds out a card printed with black, blocky letters:

UPRR.

"You-NEE-yun Pah-SEE-fic Rail Rote," she says carefully.

Four letters for the start of one more journey.

The journey to Father and our new home.

Mother pins the card to my collar—and straightens them both, of course.

Baggage at the Ellis Island Museum, 2005. In the early 1900s, people packed their most precious possessions in trunks and bundles. While older immigrants changed foreign money into dollars and purchased railway tickets to final destinations, immigrant children often piled on top of the family's baggage and waited.

Moshe and the Lady, Hungarian Immigrant and Aid Worker

(1920)

To perform this poem as a miniplay, make note of when Moshe, the immigrant, is talking to the lady aid worker and when he is talking to (and should be facing) the audience. Stage directions, in brackets, should not be read aloud.

LADY:

Are you alone?

MOSHE:

[Shakes head no.]

LADY:

Is there someone to meet you?

MOSHE:

[Nods yes, then whispers to audience.]

She speaks good Hungarian

and wears an immigrant services badge,

but what if it's another trap?

Back in Hungary, no one said

that the Americans would put me in this cage.

The guard calls this the "exercise yard."

But I've never seen a yard without dirt and chickens.

It's a trap, set to spring on me.

[Kicks the wire hard, then sits on the ground.]

LADY:

So you're a fighter, are you?

MOSHE:

[Shrugs.]

LADY:

I saw you try to break free.

You remind me of someone I used to know.

Have you seen the Danube, early in the spring?

When the water seems as gray and cold as the ground you're on now?

For immigrants in detention, the outdoor exercise yard was
a wire-covered cage.

MOSHE:

[Nods yes.]

LADY:

When I came here, I was like you.

Hard, cold as ice.

Didn't want to trust a soul.

But even the Danube warms with the sun.

Or did it stay icy cold this spring?

MOSHE:

[Forgets to be silent and answers with enthusiasm.]

No, no! It was flowing fast, just like always.

LADY:

So, you are alone?

MOSHE:

[Whispers]

No . . . Y-yes.

LADY:

Is there someone to meet you?

MOSHE:

In all of America, only you.

Please, let me try my English:

My name is Moshe.

How do you do?

Sewing lessons at the Ellis Island school, 1920s. Classes were offered to all healthy young immigrants in detention. The teacher in this story, Mrs. Pratt, was a real person who taught on Ellis Island for many years.

Paul, French Immigrant
(1920s)

Mrs. Pratt is wonderful, marvelous.

Merveilleuse.

If my dear mother could meet her, certainly she would agree.

Not that Mrs. Pratt can talk to *Maman* any more than I can.

Maman is an island away, sick with fever.

And Mrs. Pratt, for all she knows of America,

can barely manage *bonjour* and *merci.*

No matter: we speak another language at school.

When the weather is fair,

we dig in the sand and soak up the sun.

Or we climb as a group to a garden on the roof.

Mrs. Pratt points to the city's big buildings.

"Skyscrapers."

She says it slow, with a smile.

In my best English, I ask which skyscraper is hers,

and she laughs.

Soft like a bell, ringing.

Back inside, Mrs. Pratt teaches us stories, sewing, songs, and sums.

Stitches made through scraps of linen are the same in every tongue.

I'll never be a tailor—my stitches are never straight.

But someday I'll stitch a story in French and English words.

A story for Maman about Mrs. Pratt and skyscrapers and sun.

Sarah, Welsh Immigrant

(1910)

I'm knocking at the door.

But they won't let me in.

These other girls neither.

Me, because I lied about my age.

'Twas hardly even a big lie.

Anyone looking close can see I'm not sixteen.

The steamship company wanted my money bad.

They didn't look too close.

But Immigration did.

I have relatives here, I told them.

But Immigration says they're no good.

So my uncles work at a bar.

What of it?

The judge has never met them,

but he says they'd be an "unwholesome influence"

on a girl such as me.

Guess how "unwholesome" things will be back in Cardiff,

where there's not enough broth in the pot to keep my stomach fed.

Up and down the corridors here,

I've seen judges, inspectors, and all the rest.

I've lost count,

and my knuckles are as sore as my heart from the knocking.

I'm here.

I'm standing on the threshold.

But America, you're shutting every door in my face.

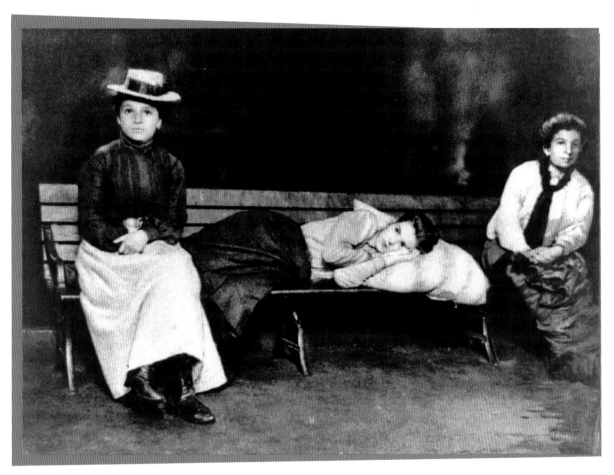

These hopeful immigrants, called undesirables, were refused entry into the United States. They are waiting to be deported. Girls traveling alone had to be at least sixteen years of age to enter the United States, unless someone responsible promised to support them.

Robbie and Moira, Irish Immigrants
(1906)

ROBBIE:

Oi! Ugh!

Moira, do you see what's in that bowl?

The one the man in white's bringing round?

It looks like . . .

No, it can't be!

Are we to eat worms?

Worms soaked in blood?

MOIRA:

Surely not, Robbie.

Why should they poison us,

now that we're nearly ready to go?

ROBBIE:

Perhaps we eat too much.

Here, take this crust of bread.

Looks safe.

But tell me, Moira, when the man comes, with that bowl . . .

What should we do?

MOIRA:

Take some, Robbie.

Just a wee bit.

To be polite.

Act as if you eat it.

But hide your spoonfuls, if you must, in your napkin.

We'll empty it later, somehow.

ROBBIE:

Those people there!

Moira, look!

They're eating it!

They're smacking their lips.

Such monsters we meet in this country.

MOIRA:

Robbie, don't speak hasty.

We got through the crossing.

We'll muddle through this.

We haven't come to these far and distant shores

to be killed by a cook.

Immigrants in the dining hall at Ellis Island. While immigrants waited, either to be allowed into America or to be deported, they had to eat. In this dialogue, two immigrants—Robbie and Moira from Ireland—encounter their first plate of spaghetti.

Pearl Libow, Russian Immigrant
(1922)

The sickness starts on the boat.

Doctors wrap me in sheets.

Cold sheets, they tell me, straight from the icebox.

But I burn hotter than the ship's coal fire.

Then, suddenly, I feel jolts and bumps.

Voices, so many voices.

A wall of sound I can't break through,

so little makes sense to my ears.

Then, just as suddenly, all's quiet.

Sleep finally quenches the fire inside.

When I wake again, I'm thirsty.

My eyes drink in sights.

My ears drink in sounds.

Where am I?

A man in white comes to my side.

Silver whiskers poke out from behind a mask when he talks.

I smile at those wiggling whiskers

and wonder, *Does he imagine I know what he's saying?*

Slowly, I understand:

I am on an island, far from home.

I'm on *that* island.

Ellis Island. Island of Hope, Island of Tears.

No one will say when I can leave.

Outside the window, the Liberty Lady stands tall.

I can't see her face yet, not from here.

But I promise you this:

I won't stay in bed.

Soon enough, I'll leave this island and take my place in this new land.

I won't let Lady Liberty turn her back on me.

In 1922, teenager Pearl Libow came to America from Russia.
She became sick on the crossing and was treated in the Ellis
Island isolation ward, where patients had a view of the Statue
of Liberty's back.

Hubert Julian, Detainee
(1936)

Colonel Hubert Fauntleroy Julian, reporting back for duty.

What?

You won't let a black flyer into your nice white country?

Well, let me tell you this:

I knew I'd get wings since I first saw a man fly.

Soon as I saw that pilot, cocky and sure,

dressed in jodhpurs, silk scarf, tall leather boots,

I knew where I was headed—up in the air.

And now I'm headed back to America, whether you want me or not.

I've got friends to meet in Harlem.

I've got planes to fly in L.A.

And I've got a headline to rewrite.

Here's what they say in the newspaper:

"Harlem 'Black Eagle' Barred from Country."

The only part that's right is my name:

The Black Eagle.

I'm a bird.

My grounding on this island is temporary.

You may think you've clipped my wings,

Mr. Immigration Man.

But no one keeps me down.

Soon enough, I'll join the sea gulls and soar.

Not all people detained on Ellis Island were immigrants.
Trinidad-born aviator Hubert Julian founded the Five Blackbirds
flying circus in the United States. After traveling to Ethiopia
and back, he was briefly detained by immigration officials,
who said his visa was not in order.

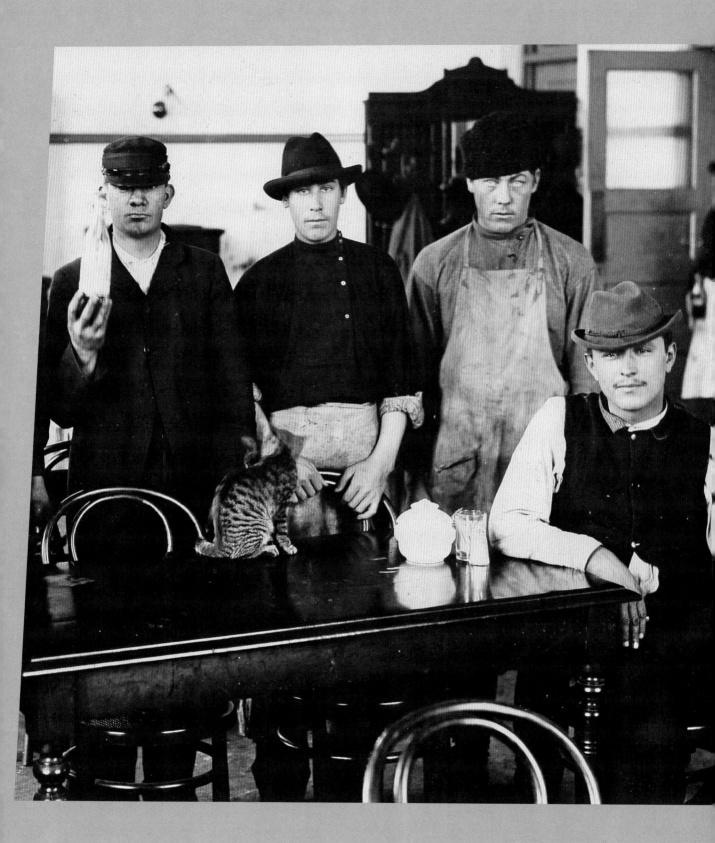

CHAPTER FIVE

Living and Working

Many who worked on Ellis Island, like these men in the kitchen, were immigrants themselves. Some, including the cat, actually lived on the island.

Like the immigrants they served, most workers at Ellis Island traveled to the island by ferry. But, unlike the immigrants, they could leave when they pleased.

More than 650 people worked on Ellis Island in 1913, at the height of immigration. Groupers kept immigrants organized. Doctors inspected immigrants and cared for them in the island's hospitals. Immigrant inspectors decided who would be allowed into the United States and who would be kept out.

Other people filled jobs as cooks, maids, dock workers, special inquiry judges, nurses, administrators, social workers, teachers, and interpreters. Many doctors and nurses lived on the island, since their services were needed at any time. Sometimes the children of these employees were also island residents.

There were frequent visitors as well, such as volunteers from church groups and other charitable organizations that helped immigrants. Sometimes film crews visited for a day or two, shooting scenes for movies set on the island. All of these people, both young and old, formed an ever-changing community, part of the fabric of Ellis Island life.

One of more than two hundred photographs taken by
Augustus Sherman, a clerk on Ellis Island, in the early 1900s.

Augustus Sherman, Clerk and Photographer
(early 1900s)

Busy day today.

Such a lot of interesting faces and Old World costumes.

When I could, I made pictures of the immigrants,

right before they shed their old skins.

"Tell her to face a little more to the left, please."

As usual, I direct the scene from behind my camera,

and the interpreter speaks.

I watch through the lens.

A flash of understanding lights the woman's tired eyes,

and she turns, shifting her children along with her.

She asks, "Will this hurt?"

I try to explain.

I will, of course, have to use a sulfur flash.

The natural lighting in the Registry Room is good, but not so bright.

The blinding flash frightens her and her children.

But it is a small fright in a day that, with luck, has ended in joy.

I collect their faces, caught between fear and joy.

I keep things in focus.

And for good focus, I need all the light I can get.

Lucia, Cook

(early 1900s)

It's not like cooking for family.

It's not like cooking at a restaurant.

I should know.

I've raised seven *bambini*.

I've piled plates with *pasta e fagioli* at a *trattoria*.

They always say the north of Italy is different from the boot,

where I'm from.

And they're right.

But the people who crowd my tables are more different than I can say.

They are the new ingredients of this country, all strange to me.

Serve rice, and some love it while others spit it out.

Roast tender pork, and at the first sniff,

some won't even enter my dining hall.

Boil pasta, top it with my mother's simplest sauce,

and don't be surprised if they act scared.

Would you believe?

They think I'm serving white worms!

There's almost no pleasing this crowd,

except in little things . . .

like bread.

A yeasty smell escapes my kitchen.

They sniff the air and know I've been baking.

So they crowd the doorway, well in advance of the dinner bell.

They stuff their cheeks and then their pockets.

Don't imagine I don't know.

I bake extra so they can take the little roll that comforts them later,

in the dark, when the babies and the wild winds moan.

Mangia! I say, wiping the flour from my hands.

Eat well.

Ellis Island dining hall before a meal, early 1900s. Cooks at Ellis Island faced many challenges in providing food that all immigrants would eat.

Annie, Nurse
(1920s)

It's easy enough to follow some of the rules.

I starch my cap stiff and straight to perfection.

The chief nurse approves.

I always ask for a pass when I want to visit friends back on shore.

I never complain, as some of the girls do, about having to live where I work.

But how can I do what the sign says?

It's nailed on the wall, right above the nurses' station.

DO NOT KISS A PATIENT.

My little charges come here so full of fear and pain.

Sometimes—no, most of the time—we don't speak the same language.

(The babies don't speak at all!)

Yet I am almost certain they understand

when I tell them it will be all right.

I smile.

They smile timidly back.

For the time they are here, under my care,

I'll give them all the warmth I can.

And when the chief nurse turns away,

do you think I can resist giving a kiss?

Nurses and doctors at Ellis Island. At the island's hospitals, signs warned nurses Do Not Kiss a Patient.

*Salvation Army volunteer, handing out doughnuts. Volunteers
from many different organizations came to Ellis Island to help
immigrants.*

Florence, Salvation Army Volunteer

(early 1900s)

Dear Josephine,

I wish you would join our army.

We have a uniform, it's true:

Long dark skirt.

Black boots, polished to a high sheen.

A jacket of worsted wool or gabardine, depending on the season.

And a bonnet, broad-rimmed and banded with red.

You'd look smart, especially in the bonnet!

And you'd love our work.

We're an army meant to save souls. . . .

But really, at Ellis Island, we *feed* them.

Every Saturday, I balance a heaping plate of doughnuts in one hand.

Sometimes, I carry a pitcher of milk, too.

You could pass out the folded paper cups.

Then we'd move down the line standing close,

close enough to feel their hunger.

The immigrants touch you, in more ways than one.

The little ones grab at my sleeves.

The older ones, with starving eyes, grab at my heart.

If you were with me, you'd catch a bit of their hunger, too.

With the crowd all fed, we'd hurry back to the army office.

Then we'd sink into the comfy stuffed chairs and stuff ourselves

with a doughnut . . . or two or three!

Yours,

Sister Florence

Salvation Army

CHAPTER SIX

Closed Doors Reopen

This abandoned building on Ellis Island, photographed in 1973, is one of many set to be restored and reopened to the public.

During the restoration of Ellis Island, much graffiti left by immigrants was uncovered.

**M**any immigrants continued to pour into Ellis Island until the 1920s, when the United States Congress put limits on the numbers allowed in. By the end of the decade, the great waves of new immigrants had slowed to a gentle lapping on the island's shores.

From the late 1920s until 1954, the main work of Ellis Island was deportation, sending undesirable immigrants back home. During World War II, the island also housed people thought to be a threat to the United States. Some of these "enemy aliens" were children who actually were American citizens. Their only crime was being born to parents suspected of spying for countries at war with America.

After 1954, Ellis Island stood silent and empty. The great hall breathed in wet sea air. Walls became soggy. Paint peeled, tiles cracked, and windowpanes shattered.

Then, as the nation prepared to celebrate its bicentennial in 1976, things changed. Researchers sought out people who passed through or worked on Ellis Island, and recorded their memories in oral history interviews. Tours were given during the late 1970s to raise awareness about the island and the need for restoration work. That work began in the 1980s, with efforts focusing on Island One.

To dry out buildings, temporary furnaces piped in warm air. And as walls dried, layers of paint and plaster began to crumble. In some places, graffiti left behind by immigrants was revealed, such as this portion of a poem in Chinese:

Lucky just to arrive in flowery flag country.

I expected peace with no worries.

Who knew immigration guards would detain us?

Left locked up without a reason.

How can we change these harsh laws?

Ellis Island reopened to the public in 1990 as an immigration museum. Although the floods of immigrants are a thing of the past, the island bustles again.

Matt, German American Boy
(January 1945)

If J. Edgar Hoover could see me now,

he'd say, "There's a happy kid."

And he'd be right, mostly.

I'm smiling because finally my family is together.

Ellis Island gave us that much.

I spent the last three years in an orphanage in Brooklyn.

Only, get this—I'm no orphan.

My parents are as alive as President and Mrs. Roosevelt.

But up to now, my folks have been out of the picture,

locked up on Ellis Island, thanks to Mr. Hoover and the FBI.

Mom and Dad were born in Germany, and maybe they left their hearts there.

Sure, they don't know who pitches for the Yankees,

and they'd rather talk German than English.

Does that make them Nazis?

I sure don't think so,

but try telling that to the FBI.

They locked up Mom and Dad,

sent me away,

and seemed like they forgot all about us—until now.

Our ship, the *Gripsholm* is kind of like us.

Before the war, it sailed the ocean with paying passengers.

Then its old life got took away.

America says the *Gripsholm* will bring us "back" to Germany,

"back" to a place I've never seen.

America's giving us away for some prisoners the Germans want to get rid of.

And I guess America's glad to get rid of us, too.

You've got to look hard to see the good in this picture.

But I *can* say it's good to be with Mom and Dad again.

It's good to see New York's skyline, too, before we sail.

And it's good to think that the Yankees just might win, come spring,

even if I'm not here to cheer for them again.

With New York City behind them, boys pose on the deck of the Gripsholm, *an ocean liner that would take them and other deported "enemy aliens" to Europe during World War II.*

Jack, Restoration Worker
(late 1980s)

This place was a mess.

It was falling apart at the seams

and soggy as the day is long.

First, we were blowing in warm air

to dry the joint out.

Then we were scraping off mounds of mold.

Some of the walls, you'd touch them,

they'd fall right apart.

They crumbled like my grandma Louisa's coffee cake on a Saturday morning.

The miracle of it all, for me, is the Registry Room.

The immigrants were so scared, I bet they never even looked up.

But if they had, they'd have seen it.

Back in 1918, they brought this guy in named Guastavino.

He was an immigrant, too, from Spain.

And he had some kind of magic when it came to tile.

Guastavino covered the whole entire Registry Room ceiling.

Terra-cotta tiles, all interlocking, and all off-white.

They're the color of coffee the way my grandma likes it,

with way too much cream.

When we started this job,

how many you think we had to replace?

Seventeen tiles.

Out of twenty-eight thousand eight hundred and thirty-two,

give or take a few.

That's some kind of miracle.

That's what those immigrants can do.

Registry Room ceiling. In the 1980s, many people worked to restore this and other rooms on Island One. Jack, the speaker in this story, mentions a real person, Rafael Guastavino, who created the tile ceiling at Ellis Island's main building.

Grandma and Jenny, Storytellers
(1970s)

This dialogue is inspired by a real story of a kind stranger who helped a young immigrant after an inspector placed chalk marks on her jacket. The marks meant that she had a disease or some other problem. Listen for the voices of two speakers: a grandmother and a girl who is studying Ellis Island in school.

JENNY:

Tell me a story, Grandma.

Tell me a good one.

GRANDMA:

I'm sure it's your turn, Jenny dear.

Here, I'll make it easy for you.

What did you do at school today?

JENNY:

Ugh.

I hate school.

We studied Ellis Island.

You know, immigrants and stuff.

For social studies.

Believe me, there aren't any interesting stories there.

GRANDMA:

Oh, you're wrong.

I remember Ellis Island.

JENNY:

But Grandma, you're from Jersey.

GRANDMA:

You don't have to be an immigrant to know that place.

I'll tell you a story after all.

I was living with my aunts in Plainfield.

We went to Ellis,

to help the immigrants.

I was a girl, as young as yourself.

Auntie Jo and Auntie Flo handed out Bibles,

translated into all kinds of languages.

You can't imagine the crowds.

People everywhere!

All dressed strangely and speaking strangely, too.

It upset my sense of order.

JENNY:

And I know how much you like things in good order, Grandma.

"Neat and tidy.

Shipshape,"

like you always say.

GRANDMA:

Exactly.

But you see, there was this girl.

She was an immigrant, in line on the stairs.

And her black coat was all mussed up with these chalk marks.

She was crying over it, so I knew it upset her, too.

Well, I took hold of her coat, gently as I could,

and pulled it off.

I knew that kind of coat.

It was the same on the inside as out.

In the early 1900s, a girl approaches a U.S. immigrant inspector, whose approval she needs to move to America.

So I turned it in on itself, to hide the mussy chalk marks.

That way, the girl needn't look so shabby that it would make her cry.

It was only later that I learned what I'd done.

JENNY:

But all you did was make her neat and tidy, right?

Shipshape.

GRANDMA:

Well, in a way.

You see, doctors watched the immigrants on the stairs.

If someone was too sick to let into America,

they marked their coat with chalk.

Then they sent them back.

I don't know what was wrong with this girl,

but once her coat was inside out, she looked all right to me.

JENNY AND GRANDMA TOGETHER:

Neat and tidy.

Shipshape.

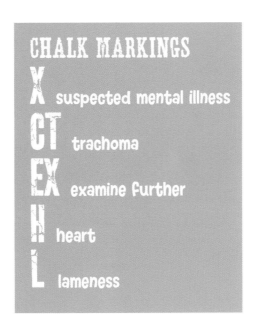

CHALK MARKINGS
X suspected mental illness
CT trachoma
EX examine further
H heart
L lameness

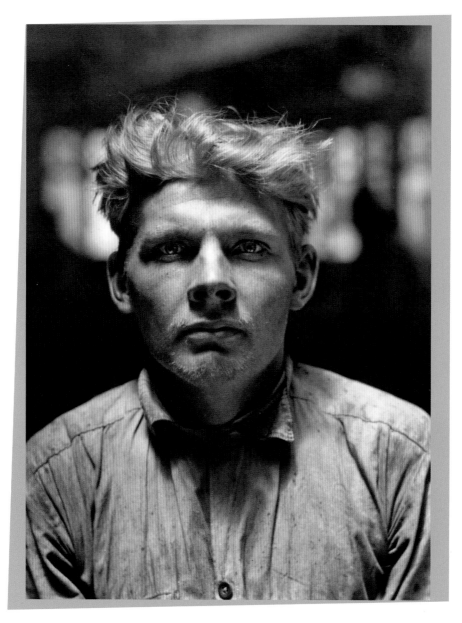

Finnish stowaway detained at Ellis Island, 1926. People today study Ellis Island through a variety of sources: letters, diaries, oral histories, official documents, and even graffiti. But some of the most powerful sources are photographs.

Paula, Student

(2012)

Our teacher, Mr. Weir, is what you'd call "creative."

That means we do all kinds of stuff for his class that we don't do for others.

It means we sometimes do stuff over.

Maybe Mr. Weir has never talked to an elementary-school teacher.

If he did, he'd know we already did immigration in sixth grade.

It was lame then, too.

"The Europeans came to this country through Ellis Island, blah, blah, blah."

"The Asians came through Angel Island, blah, blah, blah."

And not a word about people from the south.

Nothing about *mi papá* and how he went to Mexicali to bury *mi abuelita*

(the grandma I never got to meet).

Nothing about how when Papá comes back he'll have to cross the border.

Illegal, like always.

Anyway, Mr. Weir is creative.

So he has us look at photos of immigrants on the web.

We're supposed to write an "imaginative essay."

"Put yourselves in their shoes," he says,

smiling in that eager way he has.

I roll my eyes.

But then I'm clicking through this website.

He's blond, maybe in his early twenties.

His hair sticks out.

Don't they have combs where he comes from?

"Finnish stowaway detained at Ellis Island, 1926."

His eyes are shiny-bright, too big.

And do you know what?

I know those eyes—scared, but determined.

I saw them when my dad gave me a quick kiss and headed south.

Mi papá.

Promise me this:

Don't let them make you into a photo for someone to study years from now.

"Mexican turned back, 2012."

Come home safe.

Danny and Grandpa Salvatore, Storytellers
(2009)

To perform this as a miniplay, make note of when Danny is talking to his grandpa and when he is talking to (and should be facing) the audience. Stage directions, in brackets, should not be read aloud.

DANNY:

[Faces audience.]

My grandpa is a mystery man.

Sure, he has a name, like everybody else.

Salvatore Cicello.

Sure, he has a birthday.

[Faces Grandpa Salvatore.]

When were you born, Gramps?

GRANDPA SALVATORE:

In May.

Like you, Danny, my boy.

DANNY:

[Faces audience.]

But he never says when in May or what year.

And I never ask.

You *don't* ask Grandpa Salvatore questions.

You wait for him to talk.

He's never had a driver's license.

GRANDPA SALVATORE:

Why I want to drive in this crazy city?

DANNY:

[Faces audience.]

He's never carried a Social Security card.

GRANDPA SALVATORE:

Why I need money from Washington when I got family?

DANNY:

[Faces audience.]

And he never, ever answers the door if he doesn't know who's knocking.

*[Danny knocks out a code—*tap, tap, t-tap, tap—*as if knocking on a door.]*

GRANDPA SALVATORE:

[Grandpa goes through the motions of opening a door.]

For you, I always open, Danny, my boy.

Something I got to tell you . . .

DANNY:

What is it, Gramps?

GRANDPA SALVATORE:

Been thinking about the old days.

Back when I came from Italy.

On the boat, I lost my money playing cards.

To be American, you have to have twenty bucks.

In the early 1900s, Little Italy was a popular immigrant neighborhood in New York City. In the dialogue beginning on page 95, an immigrant who still lives there shares a story with his American grandson.

DANNY:

Twenty bucks?

That's not so much.

Couldn't someone lend you?

GRANDPA SALVATORE:

You want me in debt to the card sharks?

I don't owe nobody nothing.

So the immigration guards lock me up.

The beds are hard metal stacked to the sky.

[Coughs.]

DANNY:

Take it slow, Gramps.

Have some water.

GRANDPA SALVATORE:

From the top bunk, I see out the window.

Water all around . . .

So I know what to do.

After midnight, I pull that high window open,

shimmy out, and run like heck.

Then I swim and swim till I reach the shore.

Jersey City.

Took me a week just to walk to Little Italy.

DANNY:

Whoa!

You must have been superhero strong back then.

How'd you do it?

Wasn't the water cold?

Weren't you scared?

GRANDPA SALVATORE:

What I look like, the encyclopedia?

DANNY:

[Faces audience.]

With Grandpa Salvatore, you don't ask questions.

You just listen, when he's got a story to tell.

An Italian American shoe-repair man in New York City in the mid-1900s.

Lisa, National Park Service Employee
(2012)

Wish they could see it as I do.

It's empty and still at the end of a day.

Quiet, like a church.

No, that's not it.

More like a movie set after the shooting.

Only on this movie set,

the characters won't shut up.

Some evenings, the hairs on my arms stand on end.

Do I hear whispers and whimpers?

Most evenings, I'd swear I'm not alone.

The air's thick.

It's a feeling that almost takes shape in the shadows.

Maybe every immigrant who ever came here

left something behind—hopes and tears and fears.

In the daytime, tourists crowd the rooms with conversation,

the flash of cameras.

"Whoa," they say, "look at that hard bunk.

Good thing we've got a hotel room!"

They laugh a bit too loud, a second too long.

Maybe, just maybe, they catch a glimpse of what I see.

   Shadows in the dark.

And maybe they feel what I feel.

The sense that,
after all these years,
spirits live here,
along with all their hopes and tears.

Today, Ellis Island serves as a museum to American immigration.

Source Notes*

This book is based on research from sources listed below. Most of the sources are listed in the bibliography. Complete citations are provided for those books not in the bibliography.

Introduction

Moreno, *Encyclopedia of Ellis Island*: pp. xi, 143; Unrau, *Ellis Island: Historic Resource Study*, vol. 1: p. 188.

Chapter One: Ellis Islands (page 10)

"certain cargoes or parcels of goods": Moreno, *Encyclopedia of Ellis Island*, pp. xi; "TO BE SOLD . . .": ibid., pp. xii, xxiii, xxv, 127, 137. For an illustrated account of early Dutch New York, see Patterson, *The City of New York: A History Illustrated from the Collections of the Museum of the City of New York*: pp. 13–24. For an online account, see the American Park Network's "Ellis Island National Monument" at ohranger.com/ellis-island/history-ellis-island.

Chapter Two: Arrivals (page 22)

"[W]e glided up . . ." Graham, *With Poor Immigrants to America*, p. 42; also includes a good description of the journey from Europe and the arrival of immigrants. Moreno, *Ellis Island*: pp. 17, 29; Moreno, *Encyclopedia of Ellis Island*, pp. xiii, xxiii. For Annie Moore's arrival, see *New York Tribune*, January 2, 1892. For an oral history showing the immigrant's point of view on arriving at Ellis Island, see Emanuel "Manny" Steen's account of his arrival in 1925 in Coan, *Ellis Island Interviews: In Their Own Words*: pp. 122–125. For accounts of Christmas on Ellis Island, see Moreno, *Encyclopedia of Ellis Island*: pp. 35–36, and Martin, Ellis Island Oral History Project, AKRF-125.

Chapter Three: Inspections (page 34)

For accounts of the inspection process, see Moreno, *Encyclopedia of Ellis Island*: "Line Inspections" (pp. 142–145) and "Primary Inspection" (p. 193); Shapiro, Mary J., *Ellis Island: An Illustrated History of the Immigrant Experience* (New York: Macmillan, 1991): pp. 112–122. On medical inspections, see Parascandola, "Doctors at the Gate: PHS at Ellis Island," *Public Health Reports*. For an oral history account of a doctor on Ellis Island, see Anderson, Ellis Island Oral History Project, NPS-104. Anderson was a doctor in the early 1900s. For a photograph of Inspector Najeeb Abreely, see Moreno, *Ellis Island*: p. 14. For an actual letter to President Roosevelt from Margaret Batchelder see Unrau, *Ellis Island: Historic Resource Study*, vol. 2: pp. 307–311. For immigrant Arnold Weiss's oral history interview, see Sandler, *Island of Hope: The Story of Ellis Island and the Journey to America*: pp. 47–48.

*All websites active at time of publication

Chapter Four: Island of Hope, Island of Tears (page 50)

"There's more tears . . .": Fannie Klingerman, quoted in Sandler, *Island of Hope: The Story of Ellis Island and the Journey to America*: p. 64; "likely to become . . .": Immigration Act of 1891, U.S. Immigration Legislation Online, library.uwb.edu/guides/USimmigration/1891_immigration_act.html. For an account of a patient at the Ellis Island hospital in 1922, see Libow, Ellis Island Oral History Project, NPS-106. "Harlem 'Black Eagle' . . .": *New York Times*, January 24, 1936 (available for purchase at the *New York Times* website, nytimes.com).

Chapter Five: Living and Working (page 68)

For more on Augustus Sherman and his Ellis Island photographs, see Mesenholler, Peter, *Augustus F. Sherman: Ellis Island Portraits, 1905–1920* (New York: Aperture, 2005). For background on Public Health Service nurses, see Parascandola, John, "Women in the Public Health Service," *Leadership in Public Health*, and Moreno, *Encyclopedia of Ellis Island*: "Nurses" (pp. 184–185).

Chapter Six: Closed Doors Reopen (page 80)

"enemy aliens": *Moreno, Encyclopedia of Ellis Island*: pp. 75–77; "Lucky just to arrive . . .": Shuster, Mike, "Ellis Island Graffiti Found," National Public Radio. For information on the island's restoration, see Moreno, *Encyclopedia of Ellis Island*: pp. xv–xvi, and "Restoration" (p. 210). For background on World War II internment on Ellis Island, see Moreno, *Encyclopedia of Ellis Island*, "Enemy Aliens" (pp. 75–77). For stories of German American families interned on or passing through Ellis Island during World War II, see "Real People" at the German American Internee Coalition website at gaic.info/real_people.html. For an account of an immigrant turning a chalk-marked coat inside out, see the quotation from Victoria Sarfatti Fernandez, a Macedonian immigrant in 1916, in Shapiro, Mary J., *Ellis Island: An Illustrated History of the Immigrant Experience*: p. 115. For more on stowaways, see Moreno, *Encyclopedia of Ellis Island*, "Stowaways" (p. 229).

Bibliography

Books

Abbott, Edith. *Immigration: Select Documents and Case Records*. New York: Arno Press, 1969.

Brandenberg, Broughton. *Imported Americans: The Story of the Experiences of a Disguised American and His Wife Studying the Immigration Question*. New York: Stokes, 1904.

Coan, Peter Morton. *Ellis Island Interviews: In Their Own Words*. New York: Facts on File, 1997.*

Conway, Lorie. *Forgotten Ellis Island: The Extraordinary Story of America's Immigrant Hospital*. New York: HarperCollins/Smithsonian Books, 2007.

Fairchild, Amy L. *Science at the Borders: Immigrant Inspection and the Shaping of the Modern Industrial Labor Force*. Baltimore: Johns Hopkins University Press, 2003.

Graham, Stephen. *With Poor Immigrants to America*. New York: Macmillan, 1914.

Kraut, Alan M. *Silent Travelers: Germs, Genes, and the "Immigrant Menace."* New York: Basic Books, 1994.

Kroll, Steven. *Ellis Island: Doorway to Freedom*. Illustrated by Karen Ritz. New York: Holiday House, 1995.*

Moreno, Barry. *Children of Ellis Island*. Charleston, SC: Arcadia, 2005.

Moreno, Barry. *Ellis Island*. Charleston, SC: Arcadia, 2003.

Moreno, Barry. *Encyclopedia of Ellis Island*. Westport, CT: Greenwood Press, 2004.

Mullan, Fitzhugh. *Plagues and Politics: The Story of the United States Public Health Service*. New York: Basic Books, 1989.

Patterson, Jerry E. *The City of New York: A History Illustrated from the Collections of the Museum of the City of New York*. New York: Harry N. Abrams, 1978.

Peacock, Louise. *At Ellis Island: A History in Many Voices*. Illustrated by Walter Lyon Krudop. New York: Atheneum Books for Young Readers, 2007.*

*For young readers

Sandler, Martin W. *Island of Hope: The Story of Ellis Island and the Journey to America*. New York: Scholastic, 2004.*

Unrau, Harlan D. *Ellis Island: Historic Resource Study: Statue of Liberty, Ellis Island National Monument/New York–New Jersey*. 3 vols. Washington, DC: U.S. Department of the Interior/National Park Service, 1984.

Articles

Brandenberg, Broughton. "The Tragedy of the Rejected Immigrant." *Outlook* 84 (October 10, 1906): 361–365.

Parascandola, John. "Doctors at the Gate: PHS at Ellis Island." *Public Health Reports* 113 (January–February 1998): 83–86.

Parascandola, John. "Women in the Public Health Service." *Leadership in Public Health* 3, no. 2 (Summer 1994): 9–12.

Pooacha, Fawn Wilson. "Ancestral Delaware Remains Finally Laid to Rest," July 2003. National Association of Tribal Historic Preservation Officers. nathpo.org/News/NAGPRA/News-NAGPRA31.htm.

Reed, Alfred C. "Going Through Ellis Island." *Popular Science Monthly* 82 (January 1913): 5–18.

Interviews*

Anderson, T. Bruce H. Ellis Island Oral History Project, NPS-104.

Libow, Pearl. Ellis Island Oral History Project, NPS-106.

Martin, Elizabeth. Ellis Island Oral History Project, AKRF-125.

Shuster, Mike. "Ellis Island Graffiti Found." National Public Radio (July 5, 1986). npr.org/templates/story/story.php?storyId=4473936.

Wilberding, John. "Give Us Your Sick." The Story. American Public Media (July 4, 2008). thestory.org/archive/give-us-your-sick-1/view.

Websites*

"Ellis Island." History.com. View video clips, listen to audio clips, and read brief text at the History Channel's website. history.com/topics/ellis-island.

*All websites active at time of publication

"Ellis Island National Monument." OhRanger.com. Explore the American Park Network's website.
americanparknetwork.com/parkinfo/sl/history/ellis.html.

Forgotten Ellis Island. At this website, discover the stories of immigrants who stayed at Ellis Island's hospitals. Based on the book by Lorie Conway and the PBS documentary of the same name.
forgottenellisisland.com.

"Immigration: Ellis Island." Oracle ThinkQuest. Walk through the immigration process.
library.thinkquest.org/20619/Eivirt.html.
Also, take a look at a project created by fifth- and sixth-graders at Oracle ThinkQuest's Ellis Island home page,
"Ellis Island: Gateway to America."
library.thinkquest.org/5101/index.htm.

Lewis W. Hine—Ellis Island. George Eastman House. View images of immigrants and Ellis Island from this photograph archive.
geh.org/fm/lwhprints/htmlsrc/index.html.

Save Ellis Island. Find out about efforts by this organization to restore and interpret buildings on Islands Two and Three.
saveellisisland.org.

"Selected Images of Ellis Island and Immigration, ca. 1880–1920." Library of Congress Prints and Photographs Reading Room. View photos at loc.gov/rr/print/list/070_immi.html.

Silent Films

Emigrants Landing at Ellis Island. This very short documentary film made in 1903 by Thomas Edison shows immigrants entering Ellis Island. View it at the Library of Congress American Memory website, memory.loc.gov. Search for "Emigrants Landing at Ellis Island."

The Immigrant. Directed by Charlie Chaplin, 1917. Part of "The Essential Charlie Chaplin." Delta Entertainment, 2003, DVD. This film was directed by and stars Chaplin as an immigrant from Europe. It takes place primarily on board ship in the Atlantic Ocean and in a restaurant in America. Approximately 20 minutes.

My Boy. Directed by Albert Austin and Victor Heerman, 1921. Packaged with *The Kid* by Charlie Chaplin. Warner Home Video, 2003, DVD. This film stars Jackie Coogan as an immigrant child who is orphaned on the passage to America, eludes immigration officials on Ellis Island, and is eventually adopted by an old sailor. Approximately 55 minutes.

Nearly ready to leave Ellis Island and board a train to their new home, these two immigrants wait with their bags.

Going Further

— Choose a story from this book to perform as a monologue or dialogue. Dress as the person who's speaking and present the story in character as a dramatic miniplay.

— Identify different roles on Ellis Island (such as those of immigrant, grouper, doctor, and inspector) using the information in this book. Then create a play dramatizing immigration inspection. For props, look at *The Ellis Island Collection* by Brad R. Tuttle (San Francisco: Chronicle Books, 2004), a kit filled with reproductions of passports, historical photographs, ship manifests, and other documents.

— Choose and study a photograph from this book or from a website. Then write haiku poems or your own short fictional pieces about the individuals pictured.

— Record your family history, particularly stories related to moving from one place to another. Document the story with photographs or mementos associated with your family's former homes, in America and elsewhere.

— Create a list of questions, identify immigrants in your area, and conduct oral-history interviews to make a record of local immigrant history.

Index

Page numbers in **boldface** refer to photographs and/or captions.